James Bruell

Sea memories

Personal experiences in the U. S. Navy in peace and war

James Bruell

Sea memories
Personal experiences in the U. S. Navy in peace and war

ISBN/EAN: 9783337224899

Printed in Europe, USA, Canada, Australia, Japan

Cover: Foto ©ninafisch / pixelio.de

More available books at **www.hansebooks.com**

SEA ·MEMORIES:

OR,

PERSONAL EXPERIENCES IN THE U.S. NAVY IN PEACE AND WAR.

BY AN OLD SALT.

DEDICATED TO

𝕿𝖍𝖊 𝕺𝖋𝖋𝖎𝖈𝖊𝖗𝖘 𝖆𝖓𝖉 𝕾𝖆𝖎𝖑𝖔𝖗𝖘 𝖔𝖋 𝖙𝖍𝖊 𝕸𝖊𝖝𝖎𝖈𝖆𝖓 𝖂𝖆𝖗,

BY

James D. Bruell, Biddeford Pool, Me.

PART OF WHICH HE SAW, AND PART HE WAS.

BIDDEFORD POOL:
PUBLISHED BY THE AUTHOR.
1886

INTRODUCTION.

AFTER a lapse of more than forty years since I first commenced sea-life, and, with no guide but memory to aid me, the story of my life on shipboard must, of course, be lacking in many particulars; yet, with the incidents firmly fixed in my mind, I can recall the most of them in the order of their occurrence. Although a man of more than sixty years, the events that I have related in my book come as freshly before me as if they had happened but yesterday, many sulphurous with the smoke of war, and others relating to companionships that were pleasant, 'mid scenes of more quiet import. The Mexican war, of which so little is now known, forms the main feature of the work, some of the leading events of which the writer participated in, on sea and shore, and was an interested spectator of others. The facts I have given without exaggeration, and told them in a style as nearly flavoring of salt-water as I could, without rhetorical flourishes or any aim to set off the truth with artificial coloring. Simplicity pure and unpretending has been my effort, confining myself to presenting my facts so that they might be understood. If the "old salt" has succeeded in interesting his readers, his object has been gained.

THE AUTHOR.

LIFE AFLOAT.

I COMMENCED going to sea when thirteen years of age, and for three years remained on small fishing and coasting vessels, at the end of which time I trimmed my sheets for deep water, and made several voyages to Europe, until 1845, when, on the 28th day of December, I shipped in the United States navy, and on the 31st joined the "North Carolina" receiving-ship at Brooklyn, N.Y., navy-yard. There were some three hundred men there awaiting orders. Of course employment must be given them, and every morning at nine o'clock a party was detailed for shore service, some to work in one place and some in another, one field of their labor being the woodshed, where they were required to take the bark from the wood to be used on board men-of-war, as the bark made dust on the deck.

This wood business was very well for a short time, but finally some of the men thought it time for the wood-pile to play out; so a vote was taken one morning, and it was resolved to "strike,"

which was done by striking all the handles from
the axes, and when the officer who had charge came
round he found us with nothing but the handles in
our hands. He saw the situation, and ordered us
to the ship. We made little out of our act, for in
the spring came an order from Washington to send
a draft of men to the receiving-ship "Pennsylvania,"
at Norfolk, Va., and we found that all of the wood
barkers were called to "lash hammocks" and
"shoulder bags" for that destination. There were
one hundred and sixty men to go, besides the
officers, and we embarked on board a schooner that
was to take us to Norfolk. The vessel was in ballast, with a flooring over it, and we were given the
entire hold to ourselves. All we had to eat was
raw pork and hard bread for the entire passage
of three days. Some of the men thought. they
would like one square meal, and accordingly made
arrangements to procure it.

The galley, or cook's house, was on deck, the
weather door of which was usually closed. One
day the officers were to have a nice dinner of roast
chickens, that the men were determined to capture.
They accordingly placed a sentry on each side of
the galley, one of whom was to pass and repass
the open door, to see when the cook took the
chickens from the oven, when he was to signalize
the one at the windward side, who was to rap on
the door, as if he were an officer, and thus, by

attracting the cook's attention, allow the other to make off with the prize. The sentry accordingly rapped smartly, and called "Steward," which call was obeyed by the "doctor's" opening the door. There was no one there, and while he was wondering what it could mean, the other sentry made off with the chickens. He turned around to find his dinner gone, which I saw passed from hand to hand down the fore-hatch. There was a big 'fow aft, but in vain, for when the officer got forward the chickens were all devoured.

We arrived at Norfolk on the night of the third day at twelve o'clock, and anchored within hailing distance of the "Pennsylvania." The schooner was hailed by the officer of the deck, to know what we wanted so near, and when informed that we had a draft of men for the ship, in a few moments the whistle of the boatswain's mate was heard at the hatch call.ng, "All hands lash and carry for the ship!" It was kind of rough on the boys, but in the navy every one has to start upon the word.

It is the rule on Uncle Samuel's ships, as I found, that the *last* order must be obeyed. If the captain should order you to go to the purser's ward and tell him to "splice the main brace," and on the way you should meet the boatswain, who should tell you to shift the guy to windward, you are bound to obey him. If you pass on to obey the original order, the boatswain may report you at the mast.

It was so while I was in the navy, and punishable as
" disobedience of orders."

But I am running off my course, and will square
yards for a return to the "Pennsylvania." The boats
from the ship came alongside to transfer the men on
board, and it was half-past one o'clock when the
boatswain gave the order to "pipe down." At 4
A.M. all hands were piped to "up hammocks!" that
were to be stowed in the nettings. The "Pennsylvania" was a vast ship, with a company of fifteen
hundred men and boys on board, with room for
more. She was a four-decker, and pierced for
one hundred and forty-four guns. She had remained in one place so long that she had grounded
on the beef bones that came out of the men's
kettles.

Among so large a number of men as were here
gathered together, as may be supposed, all sorts
of characters were to be found: all sorts of
mechanics, with thieves, gamblers, and shoulder
hitters. While rambling about the decks a great
variety of occupation was to be observed. Some
were rigging ships, some platting sennit to make
hats of, others making frocks or pants, and in some
quiet nook yarns were being spun by old tars of
their early voyages. One I heard telling the story
of the " Constitution " and " Guerrierre." He was
on board of "Old Ironsides " as a powder-boy, and
though only about fifty years old, his weather-beaten

features, and his white hair and beard, made him appear, as he was, a true son of Neptune, aged before his time. When he spoke of his old commodore, Hull, his eyes would sparkle and his veins swell out like whipcords. He told of his being struck on the head by a splinter; and the captain of the gun tied up his wound and sent him for *more powder*.

Thieving was denounced as a great crime on board, and closely guarded against; but it was nevertheless practised to some extent. I was witness of a specimen of these stirring tricks on one occasion. I was going up the fore-hatch one evening about nine o'clock, when I discovered a small line that led down the hatchway. I stopped on the spar-deck to investigate the water. In a short time I saw what appeared to be a blanket coming up the hatchway and disappearing in the foretop. Presently the line descended from the top again, which had a hook attached. A man seized the line and descended the hatch. The hammocks were all hanging on their hooks on the gun-deck, with some of the men in them. I watched the man who held the line, the hook in his hand, and saw that if a blanket was lying loose on an empty hammock he would attach the hook to it, when, upon some signal, the blanket would start for the top. I found that the articles stolen were sold to bumboat men, or smuggled ashore in boats.

Gambling was practised in every conceivable place on board where the officers could not see what was going on. The tops were favorite resorts in pleasant weather for these tricky gentry, who continually violated the rules of the navy, that forbid gambling in any form. So boxing-gloves were disallowed, but they were plenty enough, and much trouble sprung from them, as the men using them were noisy and quarrelsome, for which they were put in irons, gagged, and, when sobered and subdued, had to receive twelve lashes on the bare back. All sorts of devices were practised to relieve the monotony of life on shipboard.

About this time trouble was seen arising from the disputed question of the boundary between Mexico and the United States, and work at the navy-yard was brisk. At Norfolk ships of war were being repaired and fitting for sea, and the new United States ship "St. Mary," built at Washington, arrived at Norfolk. The interest of the men was awakened, and knots of them assembled, talking over as to what ships they wished to go in, and what officers they would like to sail with. Men were detailed every few days to go with the water-boat to the Dismal Swamp for water, bringing some 60,000 gallons, and things began to look lively generally. The Dismal Swamp water was very good. It was called "juniper water," because it smelt and tasted of juniper. It made very nice tea.

One day the executive officers of the "Saratoga" and the "St. Mary" (Lieuts. Farragut and Kennedy) came on board to take a look at our men, and a few days later they came again to pick out crews for their ships. The men were drawn up in lines upon the gun-deck. The able seamen were in the front line to be drawn from, the ordinary seamen and boys in lines by themselves. After the number of able seamen for each crew was picked out, the ordinary seamen and boys were taken. The Lieut. Farragut here mentioned was to be the hero of Mobile and New Orleans. The officers went to the head of the line of seamen, each taking one alternately, who would fall back as he was chosen. Jack Savage and myself were side by side, and feared we should be separated, but upon saying to Lieut. Kennedy that we would like to volunteer for the "St. Mary," he said, "All right, my men, fall back!" and we had our wish. The two ships' companies were picked out, and in a few days the ship "Saratoga" went into commission, transferring her men on board.

I have thus far failed to speak of Jack Savage, with whom I had sailed several voyages before I shipped in the navy, whom I found on the "Pennsylvania." Jack and I had walked deck in calms and storms, and spun yarns of our early days. He told me of his home scenes in the old Pine-Tree State, and of his mother, sisters, and brothers,

whom he had left, to earn his bread upon the sea.
He described the parting from his mother, who
threw her arms about his neck, and, with her
motherly kiss upon his brow, bade farewell to her
boy. Poor Jack! That was his last kiss from
her, for on his return, after ten years' absence,
he found that his dear old mother had slipped her
cable and gone to rest. Jack was what we could
call a true Yankee sailor: faithful in his duty,
obedient to his officers, and kind to his shipmates.
It was pleasant to know that we were not to be
separated.

The "St. Mary" was not likely to be ready for
some time, and her company was transferred from
the "Pennsylvania" to the frigate "Constellation,"
then lying up, stripped to her gantline. We were
on board this ship for two weeks, during which the
"St. Mary" was taking her battery, shot, shells,
water, and stores on board; and we worked on
board of her each day. We liked our new ship.
She was a first-class sloop-of-war, of one thousand
tons, mounting twenty-two guns, eighteen 32-
pounders, and four 64-pounders, commanded by
Capt. John L. Saunders; executive officer, A. H.
Kennedy; lieutenants, William Taylor, Charles
Steedman, Charles Morris; sailing-master, Joshua
D. Todd; and six midshipmen. The ship's company
numbered 212, all told.

Our ship went into commission April 1, 1845;

and I heard Lieut. Kennedy tell Lieut. Farragut that of all crews within his experience he had never seen so fine a lot of men. All were Yankees with a few exceptions. In the main-top, where I was stationed, out of eighteen men, ten of them were more than six feet tall, and throughout the ship the men were of like average proportion. The officers were very proud of the company. I must say, as one of the crew, that there were some officers — two especially — that were disliked by the men, but as they have gone to Davy Jones' Locker, I will let them rest in peace. Lieut. Kennedy, our executive officer, was a little man, but his heart was as large as a thirty-two-pound shot; a man who behaved himself, and performed his duties like a man. He was the sailor's friend, and respected by all of us. Lieut. Steedman — at this writing an admiral, stationed at the California navy-yard, — was a noble specimen of the American naval officer. He was strict in his discipline, but kind to his men, and was beloved by the entire ship's company. Lieut. Morris, son of the late Com. Morris, was one of nature's noblemen; but we did not have him long with us, as he was fired at by a treacherous Mexican, while in a boat with a flag of truce, and killed. Our middies were a fine lot of gentlemen, those who are living, commanders in our navy; and our warrant-officers, boatswain, sail-maker, carpenter, and gunner were all good men. Of one officer I have forgotten to

speak, and he was too good a man to pass by un-
noticed: our purser, Mr. Littleton T. Waller, a
Virginian.   He was a most exemplary person, beloved by all on board.

Jack Savage and myself belonged to the wardroom boat.   This boat is used by all the officers in
the wardroom.   The captain has his boat by himself.   There are on board six boats.   The launch is
stowed on deck, built to carry one hundred men;
the first, second, third, and fourth cutters and gig
are hoisted to the davits.   We had some nice times
in rowing the officers back and forth between the
ship and shore while we lay at Norfolk.   An incident occurred affecting one of the boat's crew that
shows how the appetite will run away with the reason.   A middie, commanding the first cutter, with
a crew of men, went to the yard to fetch on board
the spirits belonging to the ship's stores.   The
spirits were in barrels, and they had to be rolled
down from the storehouse to the boat.   While the
crew were doing this, the officer's eyes being turned
just then in the wrong direction, they ended up one
of the barrels, took the head out, and were all
"tight" in no time.   The officer was sent below
for a week, and each of the men received twelve
lashes on the bare back, — a sore job for them.

There were several men-of-war at Norfolk, — the
" Princeton " (Com. Stockton), " Saratoga," "St.
Mary," and " Porpoise,"—and appearances indicated

that there would soon be a movement. The men were drilled at the big and small guns, and also at reefing and furling sails, and sending spars up and down. Our ship was "A No. 1" in all the manœuvres. The order came at last, and all the ships dropped down to Fortress Monroe, safely anchoring in Hampton Roads. Nothing of note occurred here except a severe gale, during which we sent down yards and let go the third anchor. As soon as the gale was over the commodore made signals for all to get under way and make sail for Galveston, Texas.

As our ship passed Cape Henry she came up with the commodore, when all hands manned the rigging and gave him three cheers. The "St. Mary" sailed so fast that we had to shorten sail, for the "Porpoise" to keep up with us. The "Princeton" did not utilize her steam, but kept on under canvas only. The passage to the Hole in the Wall was very pleasant, with fair winds all the way. We were constantly being drilled at the big guns, and our executive officer made me captain of gun No. 5.

Regarding rations at sea. Our ship having but two decks, we had to spread our mess-cloth on the upper deck, between the guns. This mess-cloth was painted canvas, about seven feet square, upon which the grub was placed, and the men, twelve in number, seated themselves around it on the deck. Each mess was allowed a chest to keep its stores in, which contains tea, sugar, molasses, butter, cheese, pickles, and dried fruit, together with mess-kettle, pots, pans, and spoons. Each mess has its cook. He stops his rations and gets the amount in cash, $21 every three months, which pays very well. The rations for each man in the United States navy are : three pounds pork, two pounds beef, one pound flour, half-pound rice, quarter-pound dried fruit, half a dozen pickles, six dozen biscuits, fourteen ounces sugar, one and three-quarters ounces tea, four ounces butter, one and one-half pint beans, half a pint molasses, half a pint vinegar. These were the rations when I was in the navy, but at the present time there are more preserved meats and less salt provisions.

It may be interesting to know, especially by my female readers, how cooking is managed in the navy. The ship's cooking-range is about eight feet square and six feet high, with two tanks in the after end, in charge of the ship's cook. These tanks are six feet by four, and four feet high, one of which is for tea-water, the other for cooking the pork, beef, and bean-soup. There are two large faucets by which to draw the soup and tea-water. The tea is not put into the tank, and half an hour before meal time it is reported to the officer of the deck, who gives his order to the mess cooks to draw their tea-water, put their tea and sugar into their mess-kettles, and go to the ship's cook to obtain about a quart of hot water for each man. These are covered up, and placed

in the mess-chest to cook for half an hour, when
about five minutes before meal-time they stir up the
tea, fill the several pails, and serve it to their men.
The forward part of the range is used by the
cooks for the officers. The tanks, or coppers, after
every meal, must be thoroughly cleaned. The cook
jumps in with his cloth and cleans the coppers until
they shine like burnished steel, and then reports to
the chief cook, or "doctor," who takes a piece of
white paper and rubs it on the inside; if it stains
the paper it is not clean. I never saw the cook's
coppers go back on him. The cook has a certain
number of sticks of wood served out to him at every
meal.

We had been out ten days from Norfolk when the
man at the mast-head reported land ahead. In an
hour's time we could see it from the deck. It proved
to be the Hole in the Wall. The "Porpoise" was
booming along with every sail set, while we were
under topsail, with the mizzen clewed down to the
cap. At 12 M. we were abreast the light with the
squadron in sight astern. The morning following
we passed the "Isaacs" with a stiff breeze from the
eastward. The lookout reported a large ship ahead,
steering the same course that we were. The commodore made signal to our ship to chase and speak
her, she being twelve miles ahead. This was the
first time that we had been allowed to see how the
"St. Mary" would go, and every rag of canvas was

set that would draw. The log showed that we were going fourteen knots an hour. In three hours we overhauled the ship, which proved to be the "Isaac Newton," of Boston, bound to New Orleans, in ballast. After speaking her we hauled in studding-sails, and shortening sail, waited for the fleet to come up. Then the order was given to "*splice the main-brace*," which piece of seamanship may deserve a brief explanation. It was usual on board ship, when taking in or making sail, if the work was performed in first-class style, and the captain was in humor, for him to order up the grog-tub and give the men a "tod" all round, which delicate operation was called "splicing the main-brace." No one is compelled to perform the duty unless he chooses.

For two days we sailed along with fine breezes and pleasant weather, and plenty of exercise at the big guns. On the third morning the commodore's ship came up and spoke us, ordering us to make sail for our destination. We then manned the rigging, gave him three cheers, and made all sail, with a fine breeze from the eastward. In three hours there was not a sail in sight. At 1 P.M. the lookout aloft reported sail right astern, and at 4.30 P.M., the "Princeton," under steam and sail, with the "Porpoise" in tow, came up within hailing distance of us. So much for steam and canvas together.

Our ship was now nearing her destination, and approaching the Texan coast at midnight, sounded in fourteen fathoms of water. We sent up rockets and burnt blue lights to learn whether there were any ships lying off Galveston. We got no answer, and lay to till morning, when, finding no land in sight, we crowded on sail, and in about an hour made the land. At 9.30 A.M. we came to anchor in ten fathoms of water, five miles outside of Galveston Bar. We furled sails, sent down top-gallant and royal yards, and spread awnings. At 4 P.M. the squadron arrived and came to anchor. The commodore sent a boat ashore for orders and mail-bags for the fleet. We heard that night that Gen. Taylor had landed at Corpus Christi with his army. The war-star we knew was rising.

After lying here three days we had orders to sail for Rio Grande del Norte, where we found the United States ship "John Adams" and brig "Somers," with transports. We lay within two miles of the beach, and while there the battle of Palo Alto was fought. We could hear the guns very plainly from the ships. As soon as the battle was over news of the victory was telegraphed to the ships, and the death of Major Ringold.

We remained here until the battle of Resaca de la Palma was fought, when our ship and the "Saratoga" were ordered back to Galveston for a short time. While lying there the officers thought it a good time to get some fish. The "Saratoga" had a seine on board, and so, taking two boats, one from each ship, officered by Mr. Kennedy and Mr. Steedman of the "St. Mary," and Mr. Farragut and two officers of the "Saratoga," manned by twenty-five men, provided with frying-pans, pork, etc., we proceeded to the fishing-ground. The harbor of Galveston has the disadvantage of a bar, inside of which are a number of spits. We rowed in on the back of one of these spits and hove the seine. There were plenty of mullets jumping out of the water, and a part of the men held the seine by one end on shore, while the rest ran around with the other end until the two came together, when all hands hauled in, and when the seine was landed there was a sight to behold! We had barrels and barrels of fish, — hundred of barrels, apparently, — about the size of ordinary herring, with plenty of mullets for all hands. We spread the seine to dry, brought wood for the fire, cleaned the fish, and sent one boat back loaded with them, for the ship's use.

One day while lying at Galveston the third cutter was sent on shore in charge of one of the midshipmen for the mail-bags. They arrived all right, but returning in the afternoon, the wind began to blow very fresh, and it was a hard pull to get to the ship. After rowing some time, and not making much headway, the men tossed their oars and refused to pull any more in that direction. The officer tried to force them to proceed; but it was of no use. Then he ordered them to ship their oars and return to land.

They arrived at Galveston before night, where the officer went ashore, ordering that the boat should go alongside the cutter, that lay a short distance from the town. The crew left their boat, dropping her astern, and went on board the cutter. The officers were all on shore except the boatswain, who had been left in charge. Jack Stubbs, the coxswain of the ship's boat, proposed to the boat's crew that they should steal the boat and run away. They all consented, and the plan they adopted to get into the boat again was ingenious. The coxswain went aft, and told the officer, who questioned him, that he wanted to go back to the boat to get his jacket. Then he slid down by the painter. The others then came aft, and all were clamorous for Jack to pass their coats, one after the other sliding down the painter. It being dusk, the officer did not detect the trick until it was too late. When he came aft the painter was cut, the sails were set, and the boat on her way up the river. They went up Red River, sold the boat, and escaped to New Orleans. As the boat did not arrive at the ship during the night, the fourth cutter was ordered in the morning to go in and learn where she was. They found Mr. Yates, the officer of the boat; but his crew had skipped. On his return with his report the captain was very angry, ordering him off duty and to keep below for a week.

A few days after this occurrence we got under way

for Vera Cruz. On the passage down we fell in
with a schooner that had lost her foremast. She
was bound to Vera Cruz, with a cargo of stores for
the fleet, and, giving her a hawser, we towed her in.
We came to anchor at the island of Sacrificios, four
miles from Vera Cruz, the castle of St. Juan de
Ulloa, bearing N.W. by N. At the time of our
arrival we found quite a fleet of men-of-war and a
new commodore, Com. Connor. Com. Stockton had
been relieved to go to California, to succeed Com.
Sloat. The "John Adams" was flag-ship, the
squadron consisting of the "John Adams" "St.
Mary," "Saratoga," "Mississippi," "Porpoise,"
and "Somers." The "Princeton" was blockading
Vera Cruz. We were called to bury one of our shipmates, who had died of consumption. We buried
him on the island of Sacrificios, with a board at his
head and feet. Jack Griffin painted the following
epitaph on his head-board : —

> " Stop, sailors, stop, as you pass near :
> Away from friends and home so dear,
> I died a stranger in a foreign land,
> And was buried here by my shipmates' hands."

One day while lying there a very large and peculiar
fish made his appearance on the surface of the water,
and John Downing, the captain of the foretop, asked
permission to go and harpoon him. Mr. Kennedy
gave his permission, and so he took the first cutter

and crew, with harpoon and coil of rigging, and went for the fish. The other ships began to send boats to see the fun. Downing was an old whaleman, and when he came up with the fish he gave him the iron. The monster started like a racer, moving round in a circle. The other boats made fast to ours, and there were eight boats in tow. He kept up the same speed, round and round, for about an hour, when he began to slack up, and finally grounded upon the island. All hands got ropes on him to drag him up for inspection, when he proved to be a devil-fish of enormous size, estimated by the officers to weigh fully five tons.

An incident happened that gave us great regret. We had to part with our veteran shipmate, Bill Fraser, who was ordered on board the brig "Somers," to serve as gunner. He was a favorite of the whole crew, who were loath to have him go. He was very interesting in spinning yarns, and possessed a great memory. He was born upon the sea, and had passed all of his life afloat, improving his spare time in writing his experiences on the ocean. It made a large book, concerning which he said: "If I live till this cruise is over I will have it printed." Poor old Bill! his cruise was about ended, for six months after leaving our ship he was drowned by the capsizing of one of the "Somers'" boats in a gale. This occurred about seven miles from Sacrificios, and was seen from the ships, boats being sent in relief; but

owing to the wind and sea the foundered boat went
down in about ten minutes. But two boats reached
the spot, — one French and one American, — three
hours after the "Somers'" boat had sunk, finding
several of her crew clinging to some wreckage; but
Veteran Bill, our old shipmate, was with the lost;
his life closed on the ocean, — his cradle and grave.

Orders came for us to relieve the "Princeton" on
the blockade. That ship the Mexicans called the
"Yankee Devil," as she cruised round without sails,
and showed no smoke. We feared we should have
a long drag at it, and our water was becoming short,
our commodore putting us on one pint per day, besides our tea-water. The "Stockton" came to
anchor as we received orders to weigh. A descrip-
tion of "weighing anchor" may interest some.
There is a place on board ships called a "manger,"
under the heel of the bowsprit, where there is a
large sheave horizontal with the deck. The messenger, which is a chain with long links, has one
end passed through this sheave and carried to the
capstan, around which it is placed, and the two
ends tackled together. There are slots in the capstan that receive the links of the messenger, and
rope or iron stops taken to the messenger and chain.
When ready for weighing, the capstan bars, having
been shipped, then heave away, with, if possible,
a man sitting on top with his violin, playing some
lively air. I have seen our ship with thirty fathoms

of chain ahead, and in fifteen minutes the anchor
was on the bow and royals set. We were now to
take our place in blockading Vera Cruz, where we
spent three months, with nothing of note to relate.
We were under sail all the time, looking out for
vessels that might try to run in or out, not one of
which we saw, except a French, sloop-of-war.
One day we made her, running down for our ship.
As she drew near we took her flag to be Mexican.
We were hoping for a brush, and all the men
were spoiling for a fight. The ship was about five
miles away, and was putting for us with all her
speed. We took in top-gallant sails and hauled up
the courses. We beat to quarters, cast loose the
guns, sanded the deck, passed up shot and shell
(grape and canister), put out the fires, opened
magazine stoppers for the rigging, and plugs for the
hull, men all ready in their places, officers with their
side-arms and pistols in their belts, some of the men
even having taken off their frocks, and everything
was in perfect order for an attack. As he neared
us we could hear his drum beating to quarters,
and were sure that we were to have a game of *ball*.
On he came with the wind well abaft the beam, his
flag, which was partly behind the mizzen top-sail,
not appearing at all, when he luffed up two points,
and we then could see that his flag was *French*.
Our fun was all up. He came down to speak to
us. His men were all at their quarters. He was

from Havana, bound to Vera Cruz : so we beat the " retreat," secured the guns, closed the magazine, and made sail.

As our water was very low, and the men were suffering for want of it, we kept off, and ran in where the commodore's ship lay. We went on board the flag-ship and made our report. The commodore gave orders to go to the Rio Grande and fill up with water. We made the passage in four days, and anchored in seven fathoms of water. A small schooner came off, and she was chartered to bring water to the ship. A number of large casks were on board, which the crew would fill and bring off, but it was so rough they would not come alongside. She came to anchor some twenty yards abeam of the ship, and to get them on board we started the bilge hoops and put two beckets under them. We then drove the hoops on again, and reeving a line through the beckets, one end at the ship the other at the schooner, with a drawing line each way, the casks were lowered overboard and pulled to and fro till sufficient was procured. We were four days in filling our tanks in this way.

We enjoyed a great treat while at the Rio Grande. One day a boat came off to the ship with a logger-head turtle, weighing about one thousand pounds, which was bought for the ship's company, to be made into soup. Delmonico was nowhere for soups, compared with our cook. After it was dressed and

taken to the cook it looked as if it would be a perfect success; but some of the veterans thought it
would be more palatable were there some spirits in
it. So one of the old quartermasters went to the
officer on deck with a requisition for two gallons of
whiskey to put in the soup. The officer was a midshipman, rather green, who signed the requisition,
and the whiskey was served out to the ship's cook.
It was put in the soup, and after it got to cooking,
and the steam began to come up through the grating
in the deck, the old shell-backs smacked their lips,
exclaiming, "That is the boss cook!" At 12 M.
dinner was served out, the mess-cooks were ordered
to draw their soup, the mess-cloths were spread on
deck, and the boatswain and his mates piped to
dinner. As the covers to the men's kettles were
taken off, the whiskey scented the ship. The captain was on deck at the time, who began to sniff,
and wanted to know if the men had boiled whiskey
for dinner. The officer of the deck explained it to
him, and he had a hearty laugh over it. He thought
that as it was cooked there would be no trouble, as
they could not get tight on that. Those who did
not drink whiskey would not eat the soup, and those
who had the appetite for rum went in for filling up
their skins. We had several turtle-soups after that,
but there was no whiskey in them.

As we had our water all in, and the men their
whiskey soup, we got under way again for Vera

Cruz, where we relieved the "Porpoise," and took our place on the blockade.

About this time we had orders to look out for steamers, it being rumored that Santa Anna was on his way to Mexico to make peace. We were to stop him if found on his passage, and one day we saw a black smoke denoting a steamer in the offing, for which we made all sail. We found that she was steering for Vera Cruz and seemed desirous of avoiding us, as we were right in her way. This made us more anxious to stop her. She was under full head of steam and attempted to cross our track, when we gave her a 32-pound shot across her bow, which caused her to stop. She was flying English colors. We hove to under the lee of the steamer and sent a boat on board. Passing under her stern, we saw Santa Anna and his wife looking out of one of the cabin windows. Mr. Kennedy was the boarding-officer, who exchanged salutations with the officers of the steamer and stated his errand, when he was invited into the cabin and introduced to Santa Anna, who produced a paper and handed it to Mr. Kennedy. It was a pass from President Polk permitting the bearer to go into Mexico. We returned to the ship, and the steamer went on her way to Vera Cruz.

As our ship's company had been living on salt provisions for a long time, the scurvy began to make its appearance. For four months we had been without fresh provisions, and something had to be thought of to remedy the evil and prevent the terrible disease. One morning, after breakfast, the painters were ordered to paint out the white streak around the ship ; and when this was done we made sail for the land, hauling down the American flag and hoisting the English. We ran within two miles of the land and came to anchor in six fathoms of water. We were about forty miles from Vera Cruz, and, lowering our boats, we went ashore, where there were some ten men waiting to find out what we wanted. Our errand was made known, which was to procure some beef cattle, and we found them ready to trade. The price was named, which was satisfactory to us ; and then, mounting their horses, they proceeded to lasso the cattle and bring them to the beach, where our boats would each take one in tow, and bring it to the ship. A strap was then placed around the horns and the animal hoisted upon deck. At 5 P.M. we had twenty head on board. I think those on shore knew that we were not what our flag denoted, but they were very kind and obliging, letting us have goats, chickens, and everything we wanted, at fair prices. About $300 were left with them. Our stock was stowed in between the guns on deck, the goats, etc., placed under the top-gallant forecastle. At 6 P.M. we hauled up the boats, got under way, and made sail for the squadron. At 2 A.M. hauled up till daylight, and

at 6 A.M. bore up for the fleet, at 8 A.M. coming
to anchor under Green Island, where we made signals to the commodore that we had cattle on board
for the fleet. He sent his boats to help land them
on the island, and at 12 o'clock we had them all
landed, and commenced butchering. We had some
of the meat served several times, which affected the
men badly, and we had to give that up as "poor
fodder." We kept one goat for a pet, and we
taught him many tricks, in the performance of one
of which, one day, he forgot the number of his mess.
Mr. Kennedy was forward and started to go aft,
when Mr. Goat seemed to think that the officer being
a small man he had a soft thing in attacking him.
He made sail to "run the fleet," and Mr. Kennedy,
being directly in his course, received a butt that
hove him on his beam-ends. That was his last ex-
ploit, for next day he was served up for the officers'
dinner.

About this time we experienced a very heavy
"norther." It blew big guns, and we had to send
down all the upper yards and spars. The top-
gallant and royal yards and top-gallant mast were
lowered on deck, with the fore and main yards across
the hammock netting, the top-mast with top-sail yard
across the rim of the tops. There were four anchors
ahead during the gale, and, after it was over, the
commodore signalled to hoist up the lower yards, top-
mast, top-gallant mast, top-gallant and royal yards.

It wanted seven minutes to eight-bells when the order was given, and, when eight-bells struck, everything was in its place, and the men were piped to breakfast. Some merchant sailor might say that this could not be done; but, with everything ready and plenty of men, as on a man-of-war, it was easily performed. After a few days the commodore ordered our ship to blockade Tampico. We made sail and proceeded to our destination. We found the "John Adams" there, the commodore having changed his flag to the "Cumberland." The day after we arrived we had a severe norther. The day before the gale was beautiful, with not a cloud to be seen in the sky. The peak of Orizaba was in view some twenty-five leagues from the coast, in lat. 19° 3'. This mountain burst forth in 1545, and continued in action twenty years, since which time there has been no appearance of combustion. Its height is 17,176 feet above the level of the sea. To the north of Orizaba is Cofre de Pezote, 13,992 feet above sea level. These mountains upon the morning of the gale were very bright, and the old sailors said, as they gave a hitch to their pants and turned their quids over, "Look out, boys! you will have wind enough before night." After breakfast all hands were called to reef top-sails, get up storm-sails, and unshackle chains, to be all ready to slip and crawl off shore when the gale came. At this time there was not a ripple on the water, nor a cloud to be seen. At 10.30 A.M. there was a small cloud at the north, and at 11 A.M. the norther struck the ship, sea and wind together, and in fifteen minutes we had to slip or founder. We set the fore and main top-sails with four reefs in them with lower storm-sails, but the top-sails were blown out of the bolt-ropes. There were no hemp sails. New ones were immediately bent. The "John Adams" lay fifteen minutes after we slipped. She made one plunge that filled her decks with water. We set our top-sails close-reefed and hauled off. At 1.45 P.M. we shipped a sea, which carried away one of our boats from the davits. It was blowing very heavy, with a tremendous sea running, and the ship going off shore like a thing of life. At 3 P.M. we got a good offing and hove the ship to. She lay like a duck. The morning after the gale the wind had moderated so much that we made sail to get to our anchorage again, and by 12 M. we had all sail set. We spoke an English man-of-war brig bound for Tampico. At 2 P.M. we made the land, and at 4.30 picked up our boat, which we had lost, all right. At 6 o'clock we reached our anchorage, and soon found the buoy to our chains. The "John Adams" did not arrive till the morning following.

Tampico Bar is situated in lat. 22° 15′ 56″ N., and long. 97° 50′ 18′ W., and the entrance of the river is, I think, the most dangerous I have ever seen. The general depth of water on the Bar is from eight to fourteen feet, and the strong run of the river coming out and meeting the surf makes one continuous sheet of broken water, the Bar being composed of quicksands, that shift with every gale of wind. Even with a fine day, and smooth water at the anchorage, the Bar has a very alarming appearance to a stranger. Much greater danger is incurred when rowing out with a boat than going in, and coming out with the wind blowing in ; one should consider well before attempting it, for should he be prevented from pulling out by a heavy sea and wind he will find great difficulty in getting back against the current of the river, and " winding " the boat is attended with greater danger than all the rest. Within the river are from three to five fathoms of water, and it is about three-quarters of a mile wide. It is navigable for some ninety miles from its entrance, and about five and a half miles up is the old village of Tampico, on the south side of the river.

The " John Adams " went to Pensacola for water and provisions, leaving us alone on the blockade. While sounding about we found a shoal spot of seven fathoms, with a rocky bottom, and it was thought it might prove a good place for fish. Some conchs for bait were procured from spits, and we struck out for the ledges. With baited hooks we threw over for a bite, and did not have to wait long. In about an hour we had all we wanted, of a kind

called red-fish. Mr. Russell, the officer of the
boat, got one on that he could not haul. The crew
bent on and captured it. It weighed fifty-pounds.

The blockade was tedious without company, but
the monotony was relieved one morning by the sight
of a small skiff with one man in it rowing for our
ship. He came alongside, and proved to be an
Englishman from Tampico, who reported that the
Mexicans were fitting out three gun-boats at that
port, mounting one long 24-pounder each, and
carrying forty men. They were to guard the river
entrance. We had seen men building up fortifications of sand-bags, and the man informed us that
they were to aid the gun-boats in their defence of the
river, which was very narrow at the entrance. A
few days after this the gun-boats came down and took
their stations. They were beauties, of about one
hundred and twenty-five tons each, schooner rig,
built in New York three years before.

The officers kept chaffing the captain to cut them
out, and after a while he gave his consent to this.
The cutlasses were ground up, and every thing got
ready for active service. We were about five miles
from the mouth of the river, and one dark night we
hove up anchor and dropped in as near as the
water would allow, about two and a half miles from
the gun-boats. We hoisted out the launch, and
placed the 12-pound gun in her upon a slide, then
the first, second, and third cutters,— four boats in

all,— with crews amounting to sixty-five men. Mr.
Kennedy had the third cutter, with the Englishman
as pilot, with twelve men, myself included. We
were to find the channel, and the rest of the boats
were to follow us. Mr. Steedman had charge of
the launch, with twenty-five men ; two midshipmen
and Mr. North, the carpenter, were in the first
cutter, with eighteen men ; and one midshipman,
with Mr. Todd, the sailing-master, twelve men, and
boatswain, all armed with cutlasses and pistols, in
the second. Our orders were to board on each side,
forward and aft. At 10 P.M., all being ready,
we started with muffled oars, Mr. Kennedy taking
the lead. After rowing around for an hour we
found the entrance to the river. It was so dark
that we could not see a boat nor hear one. The
current was running very strong from the river, but
it was smooth on the bar. We lay on our oars for
a short time, to see if the rest of the boats would
come up, and we had to remain very quiet, that we
might not alarm the enemy. We were within but a
short distance of a battery at the point we had to
pass. We here saw a light in the launch astern,
which had got aground on the bar. The sentry
on the point saw the light and gave the alarm.
We were so near that we could hear the enemy
talk and their officers give orders. Mr. Kennedy
gave the order to give way with a will. We had
to pass within fifteen yards of this fort, garrisoned

by five hundred men in and around it, and when we were abreast of it they let us have it, grape and canister, together with musketry. It being very dark, and we so near the beach, the shot went over us, with the exception of one musket-ball that went through the boat under the bow. In a few minutes we were by the fort, and between the fort and gun-boats. Firing commenced from the gun-boats at the fort and from the fort at the gun-boats, the former thinking we had possession of the fort, and the latter that we had captured the gun-boats, and were firing to prevent our getting out with them. We rested upon our oars and let them blaze away at each other, their shot passing over our heads quite briskly. We waited half an hour for the boats to come up, but they did not make their appearance, and as we could not take three gun-boats with our one crew, and it was getting very hot for us, Mr. Kennedy gave orders to turn the boat and "give it to her." We had the tide in our favor, and she fairly flew out by the fort. They again let drive at us, but did not do any harm.

As we got by we met Mr. Steedman in the launch, coming in like a steamboat. Mr. Kennedy hailed him, and told him that it was of no use to go in, as the enemy were on the alert. Mr. Steedman replied, "I don't care a d—. I am going to have one shot at them." He ordered the launch rowed to the shore, bow on, and gave them the

12-pounder, loaded to the muzzle with musket-
balls. They did not return the fire, having all
skedaddled and left the fort. We did not know the
fact at the time. We then rowed out to the ship,
and, as we passed over the bar, we fell in with the
other boats, ashore on the spits. When we got
alongside, the captain was on deck, and, as he
listened to the report of the failure of the expedition,
he was the maddest of the lot. The surgeon had
all his instruments ready, with his bandages at
hand, but no one had received a scratch.

It was now 3 o'clock A.M., and all hands were
called to get the stream anchor out astern to bring
the ship broadside on the gun-boats. The two starboard shell guns were shifted over to the port side,
thus bringing four shell guns to bear upon them.
As daylight made its appearance we could see the
gun-boats' crews standing by their guns, ready, as
it seemed, to commence the ball. At 5 A.M. the
drums beat to quarters. We opened with the first
battery, but it was a long range for our 32-
pounders, — some two miles and three-quarters.
The shot would pass over them, but it was too
far for a direct shot with our three 32s, so we commenced with the shell guns. All of this time they
were firing at us; but their shots flew over our
ship, not one hitting her. The first shell from the
ship burst a short distance beyond the gun-boats,
the second burst close alongside, the third one

landed on the bow of one of the gun-boats, taking the bowsprit and foremast out of her. Upon this they all cut their cables and went up stream as fast as the wind could carry them, taking the wounded one in tow. After this we hove up anchor and moved off to our old berth.

In about twenty days the "John Adams" arrived from Pensacola to relieve us, in order that we might go to that port on a like errand. She brought our mail-bags, the receipt of which gives the greatest joy to the sailor away from home, tied up as we had been for a year. We revelled in letters, and papers from all parts of the country. Mr. Waller, the purser, let me have all his papers to read. He was always very kind to me, and whenever I wanted a book or paper he would send me to his room to get whatever I wanted.

We got under way and made sail for Pensacola, where we arrived in three days. We found the commodore there. We came to anchor the first of the evening, and on a man-of-war coming to anchor there is always a man stationed in the fore channels to "stream the buoy." Jacob Ambrister was stationed at the buoy, — a perfect dare-devil of a fellow, a good sailor and shipmate, but who would run the risk of losing his life for a pint of rum. When Mr. Kennedy gave the order to stream the buoy and let go the anchor, Jacob went with them. Only a few were aware that Jake had gone ashore to get some rum, in spite of sharks, with which the harbor was full. Hammocks were piped down at 9 P.M., and all hands turned in. I did not know what time it was in the night when I was awakened by the rattling of tin pots, denoting that Jack had swam on board with skins full of rum wound round him. He and his friends had a "good time" that night, but were very quiet.

As the commodore had taken all the water from the water-boat we had to go on a water-expedition. There was a steamboat at the yard employed at times for such expeditions, and so we manned her, fired up, took the water-boat in tow, and started up the river about forty miles. We were three days in filling the tank and getting back to the ship.

The flag-ship went up to town, that the crew might have "liberty." There was a circus that stopped at Pensacola navy-yard, and our ship sent one watch on shore to see it, but I think not one attended the show. Every man made sail for town, that is nine miles from the yard. I was one of the watch, and we started off for Pensacola as soon as we landed. There were several small streams to cross before we reached the town, over which we were ferried in flat boats. We arrived in town about nine o'clock, and found the men from the "Mississippi" on "liberty." They had appropriated all the hall there was in the place, and when we came to the door, finding them all three sheets in the wind, and the other one shivering, our

boys thought it best to " clean them out," so we took
charge ; but they had eaten up everything that was
in the house, and we got the proprietor to buy us
some coffee, while we went to the bake-house and
bought that out.   By this time some of the men
were getting pretty full of fire-water.   With the
coffee and gingerbread we had bought we had quite
a feast, but before we got through with our supper
several of the party were thrown upon their beam-
ends who did not right till some of their rum ballast
was hove out.   Those who kept sober had a very
pleasant time ; but there was no sleep for any of us.
In the morning we made sail for some grub, finding all we wanted to eat and some nice bouquets of
flowers.   In the afternoon we saw the launch coming
for us.   We went to the wharf, and on calling the
roll it was found that six were missing.   Every man
was sober, and each had a large bouquet.   When
we went over the side of the ship the officers laughed,
to see our floral decorations.   I gave my bouquet to
Mr. Kennedy's boy to put in his state-room, and that
evening, as Mr. Kennedy was under the top-gallant
forecastle smoking, he called me to him, and giving
me two nice cigars, thanked me for the flowers.

Having about all of our stores on board, and the
water-tanks filled, the commodore sent word to say
that he would like to see some of our target practice,
as he had heard that we were very proficient in gun-
nery ; so we made a target of a hammock put upon

stretchers, with a staff set in the bung-hole of a cask, which we placed about two miles from the ship. At 2 P.M. we saw the commodore coming, when all hands were beat to quarters. The starboard battery was cast loose, and all was ready when he arrived on board. The officers of the divisions wanted us to do our level best to hold the belt. We were to commence with No. 1, of which Joseph Fletcher was captain. He gave the order to fire, and when the smoke cleared away there was no target to be seen. It had been "knocked into a cocked hat" the first fire. The commodore said that would do ; the retreat was beaten, and he came down from the poop, passing compliments with the officers, and returned to his ship. As he left, the rigging was manned and we gave him three cheers.

Next morning the "Mississippi" and our ship made sail for Vera Cruz. The flag-ship went over the bar all right, but we were not so lucky ; we took bottom and remained aground for four hours, in the meantime a strong breeze had sprung from the N.E. At 2 P.M. we came off, and on the third day out we sighted the "Mississippi," arriving two hours before her. We came to anchor in the roadstead of Anton Lizardo, distant twelve miles from Vera Cruz. It is formed by various shoals and reefs, with island channels between them, and is of very easy access, especially when a fresh wind causes the sea to break on the shoals. These shoals, although they afford no shelter against the winds, break off the sea so much that ships ride very securely 'at their anchors, even during the hardest northerly gales. The anchorage is spacious, and fit for every class of vessels, for which reason, and because it is to leeward north of Vera Cruz a thorough knowledge of it is of the utmost importance to those who cannot reach that part with northerly winds.

The saddest incident of my whole experience occurred here. A noble man and shipmate lost his life by letting his passion run away with him. We were at quarters one day, and after we had been inspected by the officers the second part of our gun's crew, as was the rule, was ordered to the port side to rub the guns off. Samuel Jackson, the second captain of my gun, had to see this order complied with by his crew. When we mustered at quarters we were required to wear shoes, that were to be taken off when the muster was over; and the orders were strict that nothing should be put under the guns. Jackson took his shoes off and put them under the breast of the gun, and when Mr. Taylor, the officer of our division, went over to the port side to inspect the guns, he found Jackson's shoes, which he took out and threw overboard. Jackson said, "Them are my shoes." The officer made some reply that Jackson did not like, who knocked him down, and when he got up he knocked him down again, blacking both of his eyes. The officers inter-

fered, and Jackson was arrested and put in irons.
He was in irons a month before he was tried by
court-martial, was found guilty, and sentenced to be
hanged at the yard-arm. *

It is death, by the laws of the navy, to strike
an officer. The law was read to us on the first.
Sunday of every month, so every man fully understood it. A petition was signed on every ship for
Jackson's pardon ; but Mr. Taylor was bound to have
him hanged. He was confined for three months before his sentence was executed, and when the day came
the yellow flag was hoisted at the fore. Then was
heard that doleful sound : *"All hands witness pun-
ishment !"* He was to be hanged at the fore yard-arm,
and a line was led in from the end of the yard to the
slings, where it was riven through a block, and ten
32-pound shot were attached to it, and a line rove
through the same block that held the shot, which
came down, and was drawn across the muzzle of No.
1 gun, so that when the gun was fired it would cut
the line, letting the weight down and carrying the
man up.

Jackson was brought up from the berth-deck with
his arms tied to his side. The captain was on deck,
with tears in his eyes and the death-warrant in his
hand. Jackson walked up before him, and looked
him straight in the eye while he was reading the
warrant. ·He was a noble specimen of manhood : in
height about five feet ten inches, dark hair and eyes,

and weighed one hundred and ninety pounds. He
had been below so long that the tan had faded from
his cheeks. We hoisted signals that all was ready,
and every eye was on the flag-ship, expecting to see
a signal for reprieve. The answer came that the
execution was to proceed. After the death-sentence
was read to him Jackson went to the main fife-rail,
and said: "Shipmates, I will pray for you all."
I think there was no prayer ever offered up so
effective as that which he made. There was not a
dry eye in the ship. When he had finished, he said,
—"I am ready," walked forward, and took his place
on the platform over the gun. He was as calm as
death, and remained so as the noose was placed
about his neck and the cap drawn over his eyes.
His last words were " God have mercy on my soul ! "
the gun was fired, and he was in eternity. His
body was placed in a coffin and buried on Green
Island, from which it was taken two years later
to the States, in a schooner sent from New York,
where it was claimed as that of the son of an Irish
duke, Jackson being merely his "purser" name.

There was a gloom that hung over our ship for
days after the execution. It did not appear like the
same ship. The men seemed morose, and I think
the officers were alarmed at their appearance when
they came forward. After dark they invariably
took lanterns with them.

There came rumors of changes both on shore and

sea : that Gen. Scott was coming to take Vera Cruz,
and Com. Perry to take charge of the fleet. We
received orders to be ready to go up the coast to
Cape Roxo, Lobos Island. Gen. Scott's army was
to be landed on Lobos Island for discipline. This
island is in lat. 21° 26′ N., lon. 16° 45′ W. of
Vera Cruz. From the north side a great rocky
shoal extends, which leaves a strait of only three
miles width between it and Blanquilla. In the
middle of this strait is a shoal, which requires the
utmost caution in passing through. To the south-
west of Lobos there is an excellent anchorage, well
sheltered from the northers, which requires no par-
ticular instructions to reach. It was here that the
transports came with the troops, and where we had
orders to go. When we arrived at Lobos there
were two ships with troops, and another arrived
several hours later with surf-boats stowed in the
hold. We went on board to help hoist the boats
out. The deck-frame was sawed off, with a level
edge all round, and bolts passed through to hold the
planks in their places. We had to erect purchases
to hoist the decks up in sections in order to get the
boats out, which were very large, each designed to
carry a hundred men. With these the troops
were landed on the island. Sappers and miners
were sent ahead to clear up the ground, which was
all covered with bushes, and as they made room the
soldiers began to pitch their tents. Our ship's com-

pany continued to land the troops and stores until it began to look like an army camp, with a nice parade-ground cleared away for drilling. Two more ships arrived during the day, and we had all we could do day and night to discharge them. Two ships left in the meantime for New Orleans. Six remained and two more were expected.

One night about this time the sentry hailed a boat that was coming towards the ship. The crew replied that they were shipwrecked sailors. They came on board and reported that they had been wrecked about twenty miles to the north. Their ship had run on shore with one hundred and forty soldiers and sixty tons of powder and other munitions of war on board. The ship's boats had landed the soldiers, on the beach, with their arms and tents, and they had come down to Lobos for help. They were afraid the Mexicans would board the ship and plunder her if we did not get there soon. So we got under way and took a schooner, with one hundred and fifty riflemen on board, and started.

At 10 A.M. we sighted the ship, stern on to the beach, with all sail set. We came to anchor about one mile from her, and could see tents on the beach with quite a number of men about them. Some were on horses on the hills back of the beach armed with lances. We hoisted out the launch and put the 12-pounder in her, well loaded with grape, and rowed for the ship, which was about one hundred yards from shore. We could not see any of our soldiers, and we expected they were all prisoners or had been killed. It was very smooth on the beach, and we rowed alongside the ship and went on board. They began to fire at us from the shore, and Mr. Kennedy went up to the main-top, with his glass, to see if our soldiers were anywhere in sight. They commenced firing at him, when he ordered us to drop the launch under the stern and give them a taste of grape. As soon as the Mexicans saw the tarpaulin hauled off the gun they began to run to the hills. The men on the schooner were wild to go on shore and have a hack at them, but the officers thought it best not to do so, as we wanted to find out where the soldiers were.

After Mr. Kennedy came down he ordered us to get all the oil and spirits we would find on board, turn it on the sails and about the decks and set her on fire. This we did, and she began to burn pretty lively. We returned to the boat, and, hoisting a flag of truce, rowed to the shore. In a few minutes a man with a white flag came to the boat. We had an interpreter, who asked the man where the soldiers were who came on shore. He replied that they had gone to Tampico the night before. He said there was a sick soldier in one of the tents and we had better take him along. So he was taken to the boat and we carried him to the ship. All this time the ship was burning briskly, and we hurried away before the fire should reach the powder. We rode to our ship, hoisted in the launch, weighed anchor, made sail, and worked off shore away from the burning ship. At 5.30 P.M. she blew up. It was a grand sight. One mast went into the air fully one hundred feet; and she went all to atoms. The ship hailed from Bath, and I think her name was the "Acapulco." We returned to Lobos Island, where were encamped thirteen thousand men.

A few days after, the fleet came up from Vera Cruz to take Tampico, consisting of ships "Princeton," "Saratoga," "Portsmouth," "Raritan," "Potomac," and "Spitfire" and "Vixen" gun-boats. Our ship joined the fleet, and all immediately sailed for Tampico, off which they arrived next morning. Only three of the steam gun-boats were to go in, as there was not water enough, and the large ships sent their boats, well equipped. The "Princeton" took lead, with the "Spitfire" and "Vixen" in line, with all the ship's boats, containing some three hundred men, made fast alongside. When all was ready we started, and, as we neared the Bar, the "Princeton" fired her big gun, loaded with shell, which landed on the shore but awakened no reply. We had to pass a battery of thirteen guns, and expected that we should have to storm it before the gun-boats could pass. As we drew near, all eyes were upon it, expecting to receive a broadside. The big gun was trained upon

it, but when we came close to it there were neither
guns nor men to be seen in the fort, and we steamed
up by it without a shot. A short distance above we
were met by the authorities with a flag of truce,
who surrendered the town without firing a gun.
We went up abreast of the town and came to anchor.
The three gun-boats that we had tried to cut out
were lying there all stripped, with no sails bent and
no guns mounted. Our boat made for one of them,
and the officers sent on shore for the sails, which
were speedily sent off. We bent them, and remained
on board that night. We found, next morning,
her armament hidden away up the river, which we
mounted again, and then took the vessel out to the
fleet ; from there it was sent down to Vera Cruz.

The fleet was ordered back to Lobos Island to
reëmbark the troops for Vera Cruz. We arrived
at the island next morning, and the troops gave us
three cheers as we came to anchor. They were
eager and anxious to be at the front. The boats of
all the ships were hoisted out to convey the men on
board. The ships, with the surf-boats, had been
ordered to Vera Cruz, to be in readiness to land the
troops, and we were eager to get them on their way
in time. We were to commence at midnight, and
the men went to their tents at dark to rest until
that hour. At twelve the drums began to beat the
retreat, and at the same time the boatswains and
their mates, on all the ships, were piping up all

hands. In a very short time the boats were ready and sent to the island, which was quite near. It was fun to the blue-jackets to see the soldiers tumble in and out of the boats. Each ship was to take all that was prudent, but still we were to take the whole thirteen thousand. By daylight we had them all on board, and the island was deserted by the living; but there were a few left, who will remain till the last summons shall call " All hands ! "

As soon as the confusion had subsided we got under way and made all sail for Anton Lizardo, four miles south-east of Vera Cruz. We had about forty miles to run, with a fresh north-east breeze blowing. At seven-bells we were piped to breakfast, with one thousand men added to our ship's company ; but there was enough for all. The soldiers liked the change very much. At 10.30 we made the castle of St. Juan de Ulloa, and at 12 M. we came to anchor.

The ships had all arrived with the troops in good trim, having on board our new commodore, Perry, and Gen. Scott. This was the 9th of March, 1847, a most important day. The weather was exceedingly fine, with a light breeze from the north-east and not a ripple on the beach. At 1 P.M. the boats were manned by the blue-jackets, and the troops were ordered ashore. It was a pleasant sight to see. Everything moved like clock-work, without confusion, the men in the best of spirits, and all wanting

to land first. As we drew near the shore, so eager
were they, they would jump overboard, with the
water up to their waists, holding their guns over
their heads to keep them dry. They were all landed,
without a mishap, about four miles from the castle
and city, the task completed at 6 P.M. A few
lances could be seen around the sand-hills, but the
troops were not molested who slept on the beach all
night.

The United States flag was planted on the shore
in full view of the castle and city, and appearances
indicated a brisk time in a few days. War material
and provisions were landed by the ships' companies,
and the gunboats "Vixen" and "Spitfire" went up
to the castle to reconnoitre. As they steamed up
towards the castle the Mexicans opened fire upon
them, the shot striking all around them. Capt.
Tatnal, of the "Spitfire," returned the fire, and hove
several shells into the city. The Mexicans fired
upon the gun-boats with all the guns that could be
brought to bear, and it was quite amusing as well as
exciting to see the gun-boats lying there with the
shot and shell falling around them, until the commodore hoisted signals for them to return.

Gen. Scott had a battery erected in the rear of
the city, which was to be the naval battery, and we
had orders to dismount No. 7 gun (the one that I
was captain of) to be sent on shore. This was to
be followed by eight other guns from our ship, and

each ship of the eight composing the fleet was to send a 64-pound siege-gun to the naval battery, with thirty men to each gun. The crew of each gun on shipboard is fifteen, so we took the crew of No. 8 to add to that of No. 7, — thirty in all. John Harrington was first captain of No. 8, Jack Savage, second, and William Dority second of No. 7, which I had charge of. When the battery was ready for the guns we took one of the surf-boats alongside, hoisted the gun up and lowered it into the boat. It was very rough on the beach, so we took a coil of rigging and a 50-pound anchor, and, rowing in back of the breakers, we let go anchor and gave way for the beach, paying away on the line. This was to enable us to haul the boat off again. We landed all right, but the large wheels employed in transferring cannon to places where they can be used would not go over our boat, so Mr. Kennedy called for an axe with which we cut a hole in her side. A rope was bent on to the wheels, and by the strength of fifteen hundred men the gun was drawn through the opening. With the broadside of our boat cut away, we had to take another, in order to get on board. They were twenty-four hours in dragging that gun through the sand to the battery, causing the death of several mules. The guns were mounted before we were ordered to man them.

After the guns were mounted and everything ready, we went on shore, and while marching up to the battery, met our grand old commander, Gen. Winfield Scott. He was alone, and we formed in two lines, uncovered our heads, and gave him three rousing cheers. He was mounted on an iron-gray horse, and as he gained the centre of the lines he stopped, then taking off his military hat to wipe his brow, he said : " Seamen of the American navy, you are about to man the guns that are to breach the walls of Vera Cruz. I have all confidence that you will show the nation that sailors can fight as well on land as on the sea. Show them that the spirit of '76 and 1812 inspires you to-day, and if we have to storm the city you shall have the honor of leading the stormers."

We arrived at the battery in the afternoon and found everything ready for action. Our battery was placed in front of a long hill that runs in from the country, and when about seventeen hundred yards from the city, drops off quite steep to the plain below. The cemetery was in front of us, and a few shops and dwelling-houses, but we being so high our shots would pass over them. Chaparral was placed around our battery to hide it from the enemy. Everything was quiet, and no one was allowed to mount the sand-bags, though we could see the Mexicans in their batteries. Our guns were run into the embrasures and concealed with sand-bags and chaparral. As the evening drew near and everything was ready, the guns all shotted and guards set for the night, we threw ourselves down upon the sand-bags for a little rest or sleep, and, as we closed our eyes, the thought ran through our minds that this might be the last night on earth for some of us, for in the morning we were to open with all the big guns upon the wall and fortifications of Vera Cruz and the castle of St. Juan de Ulloa. As our eyes closed in slumber we were carried in dreams back to our boyhood's home, again to feel the warm hand of our mother on our head, giving us her blessing, and brothers, sisters, friends were again around us in the happy light of our boyhood's days.

Our slumbers and dreams were dissolved by the report of a heavy gun and the whiz of a shot over our heads. The word was given to clear away the battery. The enemy had discovered us. In a very few minutes the chaparral and bags of sand were removed from the embrasures, the men, stripped to their waists, each at his station waiting the word to fire. The enemy had opened from all his batteries, the shot flying over our heads as thick as hailstones, plunging into the sand-banks in the rear of our gun and rolling down. At 5 A.M. the order was given to open the ball with our battery of eight guns with solid shot. There were some three hundred guns directed at us. About 10 A.M. Gen. Scott and staff, Com. Perry, and other officers of the army and navy were in our battery. The Commodore wanted to see how the boys were getting along. Gen. Scott told the officer of our division that if he had to storm the place he should take one thousand sailors to lead the stormers. The officer asked his reason. "Why," said the General, "they will all fight on their own hook."

The Mexicans began to get a better range, and their shot came very near our heads. We made every one of our shots tell. We were called to direct our aim at the walls of the city. We could see the fragments of stone fly in every direction where the shot struck, the stone being a soft coral. As I was captain of the gun part of the time the boys would say, "Give that steeple a shot," and if the officer in command was not looking I would please them. The pieces could be seen to fly, which the boys greatly enjoyed. Our gun began to get very hot, and it required two men, with swabs, to cool it off. Before noon we had silenced a number of their guns. At 12 A.M. a part of the gun's crew got their rations of salt-pork and hard-tack, which was all they had. About 4 P.M. Midshipman Shubrick was killed by a round shot, his head taken completely off. His father, the commander of one of the squadron, was in the battery at the time, and it was a sad blow for him. The young man was a very promising officer. Shortly after a seaman belonging to United States steamer, "Saratoga," was killed. At 6 P.M. we ceased firing until morning. Gen. Worth continued the bombardment, with his mortars planted a little to the north of us, and his shells were in the air all night. Nothing disturbed the slumbers of our men in the battery before morning. Their dreams of war were interspersed with glimpses of home, — of mothers fondly blessing their children, and fathers enjoining upon their sons to discharge their duty like true American seamen. Alas! such dreams were broken by the sound of drum and fife beating to quarters. As we mustered at the gun we saw that the Mexicans had filled up the breaches in their walls with bags of sand, which the boys said they would knock the stuffing out of in a short time.

There was a brisk norther blowing, and it was quite cold, but the boys did not mind it, peeling off everything except their pants. They ate their pork and bread in silence, thinking that this might be their last meal. It was for two of my shipmates. I had fired fifteen rounds and had loaded the gun, put on the cap, and taken the lockstring in my hand, when the other captain came behind me to take my place. I stepped back as he received the string from me, and at that instant a shot came into the embrasure, striking the top of the lock, and driving it through the head of James McGinness, the crow and handspike man, and entered the breast of Jack Harrison, taking away one-half of it. We removed the bodies and covered them over with canvas. For six hours we made the shot fly, breaching the enemy's walls, dismantling their guns, and shooting away their flag-staff on every fort. One poor fellow, with more bravery than discretion, raised a flag-staff and held it up. A shot from our gun cut the flag-staff and the man each in two pieces, and the staff was not raised again. At 5 P.M. we ceased firing for the night.

After we had rested we began to have some fun. But fun, no more than work, can be well done upon an empty stomach, and so some of the men went out into the chaparral to procure something for supper. They brought in a bullock, which we knocked in the head, took the hide off, and the carcass was hung on a pole, over a huge fire, to roast. After it had roasted a while each one would walk up to it, cut a piece off with his sabre and devour it. After all hands had satisfied hunger the boys went out again and returned with several donkeys, upon which they prepared to ride. They felt elated with their prize, and, in order to amuse the officers, performed a good many pranks. One got a log of wood and a rope and went through the manœuvre of mooring a ship. He would put the animal under headway, then heave over his log, that served as anchor, pay out his scope, and bring him up all standing. Another old sailor mounted one, getting as far back as he could, and an officer asked him why he seated himself so far aft.

"This ship," was the reply, "is the first I ever

commanded, and I shall take charge of the quarter-deck as long as there is a timber-head left."

He performed some amusing tricks for the benefit of all hands, and it was dark before the sport was ended. As the darkness fell around us we sought the rest needed for the morrow's renewal of strife, and throwing ourselves upon the sand, with the heavens for a canopy, we all slept soundly until we were awakened by firing of the pickets. The alarm was given from a supposition that the Mexicans were about making a *sortie.* We each made a rush for our gun, to protect it if they undertook to capture and spike it. The alarm was general. The drums beat to quarters, and we could hear the tramp of our soldiers in response to orders of the officers. From under and on the walls of the city we could hear the sounds of bugles and the barking of dogs, attended with discharges of musketry. In the meantime the soldiers had arrived at our battery, and found that the blue-jackets had formed around their guns, with every man at his post, the guns loaded with grape and canister, ready for any emergency. While thus waiting, a man on horseback dressed all in white leaped his horse over the top of our battery and down on the platform. He looked like the Evil One dressed in lawn. He had on a woman's night-dress, and a three-cornered cap on his head, — a most unique and striking figure. He proved to be one of those reckless, hair-brained

fellows who are always in mischief, and fear nothing
above or below. He had caused the alarm. While
the boys were amusing themselves in the evening
he had stolen out by the pickets and gone on a raid-
ing expedition among the houses in the suburbs of
the city, raising considerable plunder. He then
had ventured under the walls of the city and appropriated a splendid horse, on which he had returned
to the battery. Our pickets took alarm at his
approach, with the result described. When first
seen he was on a full gallop, with his white night-
dress streaming out behind. He belonged to the
United States ship "Potomac." Quiet was soon re-
stored, and we again laid ourselves to rest that he had
deprived us of. As the dawn made its appearance
we were aroused from our slumbers, and, after par-
taking of our rations of pork and bread, we went to
our gun and waited for orders.

This was the third day of the bombardment, and
we were waiting for the Mexicans to open fire. We
could see men in the batteries that had not been
rendered useless, but at 8 A.M. word came that a
flag of truce was out negotiating for a surrender of
the city and castle. The parties came to terms in
the afternoon under which the Mexican soldiers
were to march out, stack their arms, and agree not
to take arms again during the war, the officers to
retain their side-arms. They were to evacuate the
city the next day, and our army and navy were to

form a square, to witness their surrender. This was done, and the army, under Scott, and the navy, under Perry, marched down to the western gate, from which in a short time the troops came marching out and stacked their guns. A large number of women and children came with them who were half-starved, and the sailors gave them all the bread they had in their haversacks. As they marched away we all marched in, and hoisted the stars and stripes over the city and castle of San Juan de Ulloa.

After seeing our flag thus flung to the breeze we all went below to explore the dungeons at the bottom of the castle. They were horrible-looking places, and in most of them were ring-bolts with chains attached. In one very filthy and loathsome dungeon were the bones of some poor wretch who had died with shackles on his ankles and wrists. We did not stay long amid such scenes as these, but left for Vera Cruz, the place where the boats from the ships landed. We arrived there as the sun was sinking behind the hills. It was "blowing great guns" from the north, and no boats could land on the beach at this place. The supplies for the army were stored here, and we asked the officer in charge if he had any place where we could find shelter for the night. His answer was : —

"Heave ahead, my lads ! I have a large bedroom that has a very soft carpet on the floor."

In a short time we came to an enclosure formed

of pork barrels, about forty feet square and eight
feet high, with an entrance on one side, the promised
"carpet" a flooring of very fine sand.

"There, boys!" said the officer who had accompanied us, "that is the best I can do for you."

We thanked him, and each began to make his
bed by scooping out a place in the sand to lie in.
We hove down our overcoats for a pillow, the boatswain's mate piped "down," and in a few moments we
were in the arms of Morpheus. We slept as soundly
as we would in our hammocks on board the ship.

The sun was up before we heard the boatswain's
mate pipe calling all hands to "Up hammocks!"
The gale had moderated, and the sea had gone down,
but it was only with great care that the boats could
land before 10 o'clock. We took our breakfast of
raw pork and hard bread, and after that indulged in
a stroll upon the beach to pass away the time till the
boats should come and take us off to the ships, which
lay a mile and a half from shore. About half-past
9 we saw the boats lowered away and manned,
and at 10 o'clock they landed at the beach. We all
tumbled in and were transferred to the ships. Our
shipmates on board were glad to give us the sailor's
grip, which we as gladly returned. We had a mel-
ancholy story to tell them of those we had laid away
in the sand, who were deeply missed. Jack Harrington was a true son of the ocean, and was
beloved by all his shipmates. I have made many in-

quiries to find some one of his family, in Maine ; but in vain. He came from the eastern part of the State. James McGinness, the other one belonging to our ship that was killed, was also a good man, and much liked by his shipmates. No one knew where he belonged. He came on board in a draft of men from New Orleans.

The usual routine of the ship was resumed : exercising at the guns, sails, and spars, and now and then, for variety, some man would get a dozen lashes for insubordination or disobedience. Man-o'-war duty in war time is no holiday amusement.

Gen. Scott and his army immediately started on their march to the city of Mexico, and we had news about every day of their progress. Their first battle after leaving Vera Cruz was that of Cerra Gordo. This was succeeded in quick succession by the battles of Contreras, Cherubuso, Molino del Rey, and Chepultepec. The news came rapidly announcing these victories, and when the report was made that the stars and stripes were waving proudly over the walls of the Montezumas the ships fired a salute of twenty-one guns. On the morning previous to the salute the order was given to the quarter-gunners to draw the shot from the guns, but by some mistake the shot was left in No. 9, starboard side of our ship. There was a schooner lying on our beam, about five hundred yards off, having a deck-load of mules, with a barricade on which two men were seated. The shot from No. 9 passed between their legs and killed two mules. For this mistake the quarter-gunner was broken and lost his billet.

A few days after this event it was noised about the ship that we were to be ordered home. We did not pay much attention to the report till one morning in the latter part of April, 1848, we were aroused from our sleep by the boatswain and his mates calling all hands to "up anchor" for the United States! Of all the jumping and springing on a berth-deck this was never surpassed. In the short time of fifteen minutes the anchor was on the bow and every yard of canvas spread to the breeze. As we left, all the ships manned their rigging and gave us three cheers.

It must be imagined how we felt, with the prospect of home before us, after three years of buffeting with the sea and encounter with the enemy, with merely one day's liberty for ourselves in all that time. Those who have been absent from their homes for years can tell how *we* felt. I had not been home for five years, and had heard from there but once since leaving. There were those, besides, who had not been home since their boyhood, that were past fifty years. Jack Savage said to me on the passage that he would like to see his old home once more. It was eighteen years, he said, since he had seen his old mother, and his eyes moistened as he spoke the word " mother."

"Jack," said I, "I will not part company with you till your yards are squared for home port."

"Well, Jim," he replied, "you have been a kind shipmate to me, and have got me out of many a scrape while I have been on my beam-ends with drink."

"Well, Jack," said I, "I will still be your friend; but you must promise to give me your money to keep, when you are paid off, until you are within hailing distance of home, and only drink when I do. If you can do that there will be no trouble, and you will reach home on an even keel."

"With God's help," he said, "I will do so."

We had a very pleasant passage home, and in five days after leaving Vera Cruz we made the Island of Cuba. At 6 P.M., the first day of May, we tacked ship in sight of Moro Castle, with a pleasant breeze from the east, bound for Cape Henry, off which we arrived on the 10th. It was foggy in the morning, and the ship was hove to, a gun being fired for a pilot. In a short time the fog lifted, and the pilot-boat was seen close aboard of us. The pilot came on board, when all sail was made for Norfolk, Va., and after passing Fortress Monroe a steam-tug came to tow us up. We clewed up sails and handed them, sent down top-gallant and royal yards, and at 5 P.M. came to anchor off the city of Norfolk. Our ship was soon surrounded by boats from the shore, manned by white and black

crews, to see their friends, that left there three
years before. Most of our officers belonged in the
State of Virginia, the captain's residence in full sight
from the ship. It was sad for him, on his return,
to learn that one of his children had been laid away
during his absence. Like sadness awaited many of
us on returning to our homes. Death is no re-
specter of persons or conditions, — the rich and the
poor alike are open to the common fate. Some of
my shipmates received letters from home, part with
good news and part with bad, relating how mothers,
fathers, brothers, sisters, and friends had yielded to
the destroyer. Some weather-worn old salt would
be seen stowed away between the guns, holding a
sheet of paper in his trembling hands, and reading
with dimming eyes the account of some dear friend
who had moored ship for the last time. We respected his emotion, while our own eyes watered in
sympathy as we passed by him in his solitary grief.

We were to wait at Norfolk until we should
receive orders from Washington. Next morning
after our arrival a number of black women came on
board to get "boarders," that is, to supply us with
meals from the shore. We stopped all our ship's
rations and our meals were brought to us. It was
nice to have the change from sea to land food and
cookery, after having partaken of the former so long,
and we greatly enjoyed it. Jack Savage and myself
boarded with a black woman who supplied us with

splendid fare. I give her bill of fare for one day : baked ducks, green peas and vegetables, with a dessert of ice-cream, — a banquet with which hungry sailors might well be satisfied. After lying here a week an order came to go to the yard, strip ship, and pay off the men. We hauled alongside the wharf at 8 A.M., May 18, 1848, and by 12 o'clock she was thoroughly stripped, with shot, shells, water-tanks, and everything in the hold removed, a coat of whitewash inside from stem to stern, concluding the operation. At 2 P.M. the paymaster came on board, and by 3.30 all hands had their pay.

Every one was happy to receive his money, and bags and hammocks were flying about in every direction. Jack and I paid our board to the black woman, amounting to $4. Then we tumbled our bags into a boat alongside and stepped in ourselves, intending to go to Norfolk from the navy-yard. A large schooner lay in the stream, bound to New York, and we found that she wanted twenty-five passengers. The chance was too good to be lost, and so we boarded her, and formed a part of the number. The whole list was soon completed, and she sailed for New York. Jack had kept his word regarding drinking, and had not been drunk since our agreement. There was no liquor on board, and I felt little anxiety about him, but dreaded his arrival in New York. We made the passage in two days, arriving on Monday morning. He gave me no trouble, and putting our baggage upon the sound steamer, left New York at 4 P.M. for Stonington. *Jack was all right, and I think he felt proud that he could withstand the temptation that beset him on every hand.

We arrived the next day in Boston, and in going down Hanover street Jack met his elder brother, the captain of a schooner just ready to sail for home. Here we shook hands and bade each other good-by. The last words that Jack said was : " I will keep my promise to you." I heard from him after his return home, and when, some fifteen years later, I met him, he was master of a fine vessel, and a steady and honorable man.

After leaving Jack in Boston I took the train for my home in the State of Maine. As I arrived at my mother's door I rapped, and she opened it. She looked wonderingly at my bronzed face, and said, "Who is it?"—"Mother," said I, "don't you know your boy?" What followed the reader can judge better than I can tell it.

The foregoing is a record of events occurring between 1845 and 1848, written entirely from memory in 1884.